The Evacuees

a play by
Carolyn Sloan

THE EVACUEES

In 1939, when Hitler invaded Poland, Great Britain went to war with Germany. Everyone expected that London and the other major cities would be bombed straight away and thousands of children were evacuated – sent away to safer places in the country. But there was no bombing for several months (this period was called the "Phoney War"). Many of the children went home again. However, in April 1940, the Germans invaded Denmark and Norway, and in May they moved into France.

After France fell in June, Hitler had bases close to England. Invasion was expected any day and children were evacuated again to escape the risk of bombing in cities on the south coast.

This play begins in November 1940.

Betty and Ralph Green live on a farm. The war seems far away. Their father, disabled after a tractor accident, cannot join the services. He farms and does local ARP (Air Raid Precautions) duties. Mrs Green helps on the farm and she is also a billeting officer. This means she finds new "homes" in the village for evacuees. Betty and Ralph help on the farm. They resent the evacuees coming into their family.

Joan and Martin have been with the Greens since September 1939. Their father is away in the army, and their mother does war work in Portsmouth. Joan and Martin are homesick and worried about their parents.

When the Blitz (aerial bombardment of British cities) starts and the Luftwaffe (German airforce) bomb London, there are still some children left in the cities.

Freddie and Sheila have always lived in an orphanage in the East End of London. They are not related but have become as close as brother and sister. Now their orphanage, like many large buildings, is going to be taken over and used by the army. They are to be evacuated to the country...

Scene 1

The boys' dormitory in a London orphanage.
A bare room with beds and lockers. Freddie is packing a case.
Sheila comes to the door in outdoor clothes,
carrying her case and a brown paper parcel.

Sheila: Aren't you ready yet?

Freddie: Come and sit on my case for me. Please?

Sheila: I'm not allowed in, am I!

Freddie: Doesn't matter now...

Sheila: (*Bouncing on the case*) It's no good. You'll have to chuck something out. Wear your raincoat... and this sweater, and your jacket. It'll be cold on the train. There! It's shut!

Freddie: Thanks.

Sheila: What about your model planes?

Freddie: They're going in my parcel. I'll have to leave some behind... and most of my <u>shrapnel</u> collection.

Sheila: I had to leave *loads*.

Freddie: (*Looking at her*) You've been crying. Your cheeks are streaky.

Sheila: Oh Freddie...

Freddie: Don't Sheel. Please... Look, neither of us *wants* to go.

Sheila: But Ma Blue! What if she gets bombed and we never see her again! (*Sniffing*) She's looked after me ever since I can remember.

Freddie: Well, she's got to look after wounded soldiers now.

Sheila: I know, but...

Freddie: Oh, cheer up! Maybe you'll meet a nice rich lady in the country and get adopted and live happily ever after!

Sheila: I don't want to get adopted any more. *Or go to the country.*

Freddie: Well you can't stay here. It's too dangerous now. Oh, come on, it'll be fun! We'll be able to climb trees, maybe ride ponies...

Sheila: *They* won't like us.

Freddie: (*Sighs, exasperated*) Who won't?

Sheila: Country children. Angela said. She got evacuated last time.

Freddie: Don't be such a drip! Look on the bright side.

Shrapnel: Debris from bursting shells.

Sheila: They'll tease us about being orphans...

Freddie: You don't know that. We've never lived with kids with families! Anyway, we won't tell anyone!

Sheila: (*Cheering up*) We can pretend! Let's! Let's say we're brother and sister like we did before...

Freddie: And we'll invent loads of rich aunts and uncles...

Sheila: Not *too* rich! We could have parents in the war.

Freddie: Yes! Why not! (*Acting posh*) My father's a colonel...

Sheila: (*Joining him*) And mother's a spy, a beautiful spy!

Freddie: No! Let's make her a film star! And she's gone overseas to entertain the troops...

*(They laugh wildly, then suddenly stop.
Freddie takes Sheila's hands.)*

Freddie: We're going to be all right. Bet you we are! We've always been able to take care of ourselves, haven't we?

Sheila: We've had to, haven't we?

(*Sound of a plane. Freddie goes to the window.*)

Sheila: Is it one of ours?

Freddie: Sounds like a <u>Junker</u>. It is!

Sheila: Get away from the window! Why hasn't the siren gone off?

Freddie: It's a stray... No! Here come some more. *Tons* of 'em!

(*A siren goes off.*)

Sheila: Come on! Hurry... To the church shelter. Quick!

(*Loud thuds nearby. Sheila grabs her suitcase and parcel.*)

Sheila: Bring your case... Hurry *up*! Freddie!

(*They rush off.*)

Junker: German bomber.

S<small>CENE</small> 2

The sitting room of the Greens' farm. Joan sits by the fire, darning socks. Martin is writing a letter at the table.

Joan: If you're writing to Daddy, send him my love. Martin! Are you listening? Tell him I'll write soon.
(*She sighs.*) If only we knew where he was...

Martin: Well we don't. Even Mummy's not allowed to know that! Joan? Do you suppose he might get home for Christmas?

Joan: Like last year! When we all met at that boarding house! Oh! Wouldn't it be heaven!

Martin: (*Bitterly*) Why don't you write and ask Hitler to stop fighting for a week? You could shove the letter up the chimney.

Joan: Oh, funny! But seriously – I couldn't bear having Christmas here. Can you imagine? It'll be just another Sunday like today. Up at dawn, milk, muck out, dig turnips, scrap with Betty...

Martin: You know what I'd like to do right now? Hear the church bells ring again. Walk on the downs, all four of us. And... and Prince...

Joan: Shut up! Shut *up*, can't you?

Martin: Sorry. Sorry, Joan...

(*He looks through the window.*)

Martin: Ralph's back... He's been drilling with the <u>Home Guard</u> again. Playing soldiers.

Joan: Now he'll want to play <u>U-boats</u> and torpedo the sofa...

Martin: I'm not playing war with him. War isn't a game!

(*Betty comes in and drops a bundle of cloth on the table.*)

Betty: Here's a job for you!

Martin: Mind my letter! You'll smudge the ink.

Betty: Writing to Mummy and Daddy again? How sweet! You should put an economy label on an old envelope, not use a new one. (*Mocking*) Don't you know there's a paper shortage? There's a war on! What's Joan up to? Sewing again?

Joan: I darned these for your dad. Here, catch.

(*She throws the socks angrily at Betty.*)

Betty: Right little Sister-Susie-sewing-socks-for-soldiers, aren't you?

Joan: Your dad's not a soldier!

(*There is an angry silence.*)

Home Guard: Defence volunteers of non-service age (*Dad's Army*).
U-boats: German submarines.

Martin: That was beastly, Joan. Mr Green would join up if he could.

Betty: You don't have to defend *my* dad, thank you!

Joan: I'm sorry, Betty. I didn't mean to be unkind.

Betty: Honestly! The way we have to put up with you two, and share everything with you. You don't know how blinking lucky you are to be billeted on a farm!

Joan: I said I'm sorry. What's this cloth for?

Betty: <u>Blackout</u> curtains. For the scullery, washroom and outside lav.

Joan: But we did them last week.

Blackout: All external lights were banned after dark.
People were fined if they showed chinks of light through their windows.

Betty:	That bossy ARP warden says that card stuff we used shows light through the pinholes. You'd think the Germans were creeping round the place at night like Peeping Toms.
Martin:	What? Did you hear any news in the village?
Betty:	The <u>land-girls</u> say there's been a raid somewhere, miles away.
Joan:	Was anyone killed? Hurt?
Betty:	Don't know. Oh, who cares? There's a good film on at the pictures tonight.

(*Ralph rushes in, stops and looks at all of them.*)

Land-girls: The Women's Land Army did the work of farm labourers who had gone to fight in the war.

Ralph: You'll never guess what now!

Martin: War's over?

Betty: Jasmine's had her calf?

Ralph: We're getting two more flippin' vaccies. That's all!

Joan: Two! Two more evacuees? Where from?

Ralph: London. East End slum kids! Like the Johnsons had!

Betty: Oh *no!* We can't. It's not fair! (*Pointing to Joan and Martin*) We've got *them* already.

Joan: You've still got room, though…

Martin: Boys or girls?

Ralph: One of each. And the boy's not coming in with me. He'll have head lice and wet the bed…

Joan: They're ever so poor, East End children. They get sewn into their clothes for the winter, I've heard.

Martin: And they smell and scratch all the time. We'll catch things from them!

Betty: Eeergh! I'm itching already!

Ralph: They'll be here this afternoon. So lock up your valuables.

Betty: Why do we have to have them?

Ralph: Because the Jerries are bombing London.

Betty: So? Let them stay there and get bombed!

Jerries: British slang for Germans.

Joan:	Betty! That's mean. It's wicked... Poor things. It's not funny being evacuated, you know!
Ralph:	Oh, thanks! Thanks a lot!
Betty:	We're not having them and that's that.
Martin:	You can't stop them coming...
Betty:	We'll stop them *staying*.
Ralph:	How?
Betty:	Well, city kids hate the country, don't they? So we'll make it worse. Make it so horrible for them they'll ask to get billeted back to the bombs!
Joan:	Your mum's a billeting officer, now, you wet!
Betty:	Oh yes. Maybe she's having them for the money.
Ralph:	Money? You only get ten shillings and sixpence a week for the first vaccie. And just a miserable eight and six for the second!
Martin:	That's not bad.

Betty: It's not enough! You townies, you Portsmouth toffs think farmers are rolling in money!

Joan: Listen, Bet. Our house has been taken over by the navy. Mummy has to live in a hostel, and Daddy's away fighting...

Ralph: My dad would have gone if he could! He'd fight for his country. He didn't ask that tractor to roll on him, you know! I hope this war lasts long enough for me to join up!

Martin: Ralph, you can't mean that! War's terrible...

Ralph: Only when you're out of it. When you can't do something real.

Martin: Growing food's real! It's important war work. So's being a fireman or driving an ambulance. You don't have to fight to be a hero!

Ralph: You're unpatriotic, you are!

Betty: Oh, stop squabbling! It's not even a proper war. Nothing's happening but a lot of fuss. Anyway, *our* war now is getting rid of these new vaccies.

Martin: They can muck out Jester and Maureen for a start...

Betty: I'm going to ask Mum to get them billeted on the vicar... Or *anyone* else! And you lot had better get those blackouts done or we'll get fined.

(*Betty exits.*)

Joan: Ralph, don't be so mean. They can't help being evacuated. It's awful being bunged on a train with a label on your coat, leaving everything, having your dogs and cats put to sleep...

Martin: How would you like not having any pets?

Ralph: We don't have pets. Ours are all working farm animals!

Martin: (*Sarcastically*) That cat does a lot of work, sleeping all day!

Ralph: He keeps the rats down in the barn – when *you're* asleep.

Martin: OK, pax. What are we going to do this afternoon?

Ralph: Play Blitz? Battleships? Dog fights. You can have my Messerschmitt...

Messerschmitt 109 and 110: German fighter planes.

Scene 3

The farm kitchen, Sunday evening. Sheila, Freddie, Joan, Martin, Betty and Ralph are finishing supper at a large table.

Betty:	Pass your plate, What's-your-name... Fred.
Sheila:	He likes to be called Freddie.
Freddie:	I don't mind. You can call me Mickey Mouse if you like.
Betty:	You'll have to wash the dishes. (*Sarcastically*) We don't have maids in the country, not like *London*.
Sheila:	Not even milkmaids?
Ralph:	Trying to be clever?
Freddie:	We'll wash the dishes if you show us...

Joan:	It's our turn. I'll show them the kitchen later.
Betty:	Well, do it before Mum gets back, or I'll get the blame.
Sheila:	Is Mrs Green not here?
Betty:	She's in the village, sorting out the East End vaccies. She's got three scruffy little sisters no one will take in.
Joan:	(*Sympathetically*) Ahhh!
Ralph:	And my dad's out doing war work, before you ask!
Freddie:	What, here?
Ralph:	Yes, here! He goes round half the night checking for lights, firewatching... Looking for German spies dressed as nuns.
Betty:	(*Nastily*) So *we're* looking after you.
Martin:	You ever been on a farm before?
Sheila:	Don't think so. (*To Freddie*) Have we?
Ralph:	Ever seen a cow? Or a field? Or trees?
Freddie:	'Course we have. From trains...
Sheila:	They've got parks with trees and grass in London you know!
Martin:	We have to milk the cows in the dark now. You wouldn't know how to.
Freddie:	We can learn!
Ralph:	Yeah. You can start with Jester tomorrow.
Sheila:	Funny name for a cow.
Betty:	She's a funny cow. Very sweet though.

(*Ralph, Martin and Betty giggle.*)

Ralph: Then there's Maureen…

Betty: Oh yes! She's ever so gentle, you can take her for a walk!

Sheila: Who's Maureen?

Joan: Oh, leave them alone. They've only just come.

Betty: Well they can't expect a cushy life here. Farming's hard work.

Joan: We all have to muck in. Well, don't we?

(*Joan and Sheila start clearing the table.*)

Sheila: That was a lovely supper. Real milk! Fresh eggs! Yum.

Joan: But milk and eggs aren't rationed – not yet.

Sheila: I know, but everything's short. We've had to queue just to get *powdered* milk and eggs.

Joan: Sounds disgusting!

Ralph: Know how to play Battleships, Fred?

Freddie: Yes. I…

(*Distant siren heard. Freddie and Sheila look at each other, startled. The others ignore it.*)

Sheila: (*Urgently*) Where's the shelter? Where do we go?

Betty: Go? Oh, the siren! We don't take any notice…

Freddie: But you *must*! Under the stairs then…

Martin: There's a dugout outside, if you're scared.

Sheila: Let's go then. Where is it?

Ralph: Out of the pantry door, cross the yard and you'll see the steps…

(*Sheila and Freddie exit quickly. The others laugh, except Joan.*)

Joan: They won't find it in the dark, someone should go with them.

Martin: Bet it's flooded. Wait for the splash…

Betty: Or frozen, wait for the skid…

Ralph: They took their gas masks! Did you see?

(*Their laughter falls away to uneasiness.*)

Martin: They were really frightened, you know.

Betty: Cowards!

Joan: You are mean! It's their first night!

Martin: Your mum'll be furious if they catch colds.

Betty: *You* go after them if you're so bothered!

Ralph: Let's all go! We can try those candle-and-flowerpot heater things. Take some games…

Joan: And a flask of something hot…

Martin: And comics…

(*All except Betty rush about collecting things.*)

Ralph: Get some books, we'll read spooky stories out loud. Come on!

(*Exit Joan, Martin and Ralph.*)

Betty: Wait, you beasts! Don't leave me alone here!

(*Exit Betty.*)

Scene 4

In the dugout – a basic underground shelter with bunks. The children are all sitting or lying on bunks, warming their hands over flowerpots.

Ralph: These flowerpot things are good. It's getting warmer now.

Martin: I'd rather be in bed. It smells of damp earth in here. Did you two bring any chocolate?

Sheila: Chocolate?

Martin: When we were evacuated they gave us a big slab.

Joan: And a tin of condensed milk. Biscuits too.

Freddie: There wasn't time. There was an air raid on and in London…

Betty: Oh, in London, in London, in London… I suppose you've been to Buckingham Palace and seen the King!

Sheila: (*Aside*) He came to see us. So put that in your pipe and smoke it!

Martin: (*Overhearing*) He came to see *you*?

Betty: What? Lying little show-offs!

Freddie: I heard that!

Joan: Betty! (*To Sheila*) Go on about the King.

Sheila: Our street got bombed. The corner shop had a direct hit.

Ralph: Have you seen any dead bodies?

Freddie: Yes. Too many.

Ralph: Gosh. Bet air raids are exciting!

Sheila: They're horrible. Truly!

Joan: You'll be all right here.

Freddie: Don't you know what's happening in London? Don't you listen to the wireless?

Martin:	It's bust. So?
Freddie:	London's being blitzed to bits. Last weekend the docks were on fire... Late at night the sky was lit... like...
Sheila:	Like sunset at midnight...
Freddie:	You could hear the Germans coming... A great throb of bombers. Waves of them... Then the <u>Ack-Ack</u> opened up...
Ralph:	You saw it all? Didn't you go to your shelter?
Sheila:	Our street shelter got bombed. So we had to go to the tube station.
Betty:	Tube? The Underground? You mean they've got beds down there? On the rails?
Freddie:	Oh, sure! Four-posters and eiderdowns...
Sheila:	Don't be daft! We took blankets and stuff.
Freddie:	They wouldn't let us down there to start with. Ma Blue had to buy us three ha'penny platform tickets.
Sheila:	Thousands of people sleep down there now. Nearly every night.
	(*A thoughtful pause.*)
Joan:	Is Ma Blue your Granny?
	(*Freddie and Sheila speak together.*)
Freddie:	No.
Sheila:	Yes.
Betty:	You must know!

Ack-Ack: Anti-aircraft guns.

Freddie: She's sort of... We called her... She looked after us.

Martin: Where are your parents?

(*Freddie and Sheila hesitate, wait for each other to speak.*)

Sheila: Oh, they're...

Freddie: They're... go on, Sheila.

Sheila: They're abroad. War work. You know.

Martin: *Both* of them?

Freddie: Yes. Why not? It's secret stuff...

Martin: You mean you don't know.

Sheila: We're not allowed to say.

Betty: Spies, are they?

Freddie: Just don't ask, OK?

Ralph: *Very* mysterious! Where's the rest of your family?

(*There is a pause.*)

Sheila: (*Suddenly*) India!

Martin:	India! All of them? You're not Indian?
Freddie:	(*Recklessly*) They build railways... and plant tea...
Betty:	What, even your grannies?
Sheila:	Yes... I mean no, they just live there.
Joan:	Have you been there? Whereabouts?
Freddie:	Bombay.
Sheila:	Yes. We went to school in Bombay...
Freddie:	(*Suddenly*) What's that?
	(*Silence.*)
Joan:	I can't hear anything.
Freddie:	Shh. Thought I heard a plane...
Joan:	Don't worry. We don't have raids here.
Betty:	Or visits from the King. What fibbers you are!
Sheila:	We're not! Tell her, Freddie!
Freddie:	Don't call Sheila a fibber. The King did come down our street. And the Queen. It was after they were bombed...
Ralph:	Even the Germans wouldn't dare bomb Buckingham Palace!
Freddie:	Well, they did. Twice. And the King and Queen came down the East End afterwards...
Sheila:	And the Queen said... What was it, Freddie? "I'm glad we've been bombed because..."
Freddie:	"... Now I can look the East End in the face."
	(*Silence. The others glance at each other wonderingly.*)

Scene 5

The kitchen, next morning. Betty, Ralph, Joan and Martin are getting ready for school.

Ralph: Are Sheila and Freddie coming, or what?

Betty: They've been up half the night. Mum had to drag them in from the dugout.

Joan: Poor things. Anyone seen my gas mask?

Betty: Take mine. I'm not coming to school.
I've told Mum I'm sick.

Joan: Meaning you haven't done your homework again.

Betty: I'm going to help the land-girls dig up the vicar's field.

Ralph: Going for a gossip you mean.

(*Freddie and Sheila come in, wearing indoor clothes.*)

Martin: You're not ready! You'll be late for school!

Freddie: We don't have to go until later after a raid, do we?

Ralph: There wasn't any raid...

Sheila: But there was a warning, and the all-clear didn't go till after midnight.

Joan: Is that true? If it doesn't... we don't have to go? Swear?

Sheila: Cross my heart and hope to die! It's Government rules. Ask Betty's mum if you don't believe me.

Ralph: Wowee! Freedom! I'll show you the farm.

Betty: (*Nastily*) They can do their jobs. Milk Jester and take Maureen... Show them, Ralph. Go on!

Joan: (*Uneasily*) Betty...

Betty: Why don't you mind your own beeswax!

Freddie: OK. Let's see this Jester then. Come on Sheila, you like animals. (*Aside to Sheila*) We'll show 'em!

(*Freddie and Sheila exit with Ralph.*)

Joan: You're being foul to them.

Martin: So what? Betty and Ralph were foul to us. They still are.

Betty: (*Sarcastically*) I *beg* your pardon! How would you feel if *you* had vaccies forced on *you*? In *your* house?

Joan: I'd try to make them feel at home, for a start...

Betty: You Goody-Two-Shoes!

Martin: Oh, stop it! We didn't start the war, Betty!

Betty: *You* couldn't start a fight in the playground!

Joan: Now you two are bickering! Well, we're all here together now, so we've got to make the best of it.

Betty: Freddie and Sheila won't be here long. They'll be back soon, covered in mud and blood...

Martin: I'm going to see how they're getting on.

(*Martin exits.*)

Joan: They're all right, Sheila and Freddie.

Betty: Huh!

Joan: Well they're not dirty or smelly, *or* sewn into their clothes!

Betty: How do you know?

Joan: Because Sheila's got a spare vest and knickers like anyone else.

(*A pause.*)

Betty: (*Probing*) They're not alike, are they?

Joan: No... not really. Neither are you and Ralph.

Betty: I think they're shifty. All that about India... And the parents on secret war work...

Joan: Why shouldn't they be? You're saying they make things up?

Betty: P'raps. To impress us. Like all that Blitz guff. What heroes they were in London.

Joan: You don't have a kind word to say about anyone, do you?

Betty: Oh, I don't know. I like the land-girls. They're fun and they give me sweets for getting things for them from the paper shop.

(*Martin comes in, worried.*)

Martin: Joan, Mrs Green wants to see us. Now.

Joan: Oh, right. Nothing's wrong, Martin? Is there?

Martin: Search me. She sounded a bit odd.

Betty: You've probably mucked up the milking pans again.

(*Martin and Joan exit. Ralph comes in with Sheila and Freddie, rumpled and dirty.*)

Betty: You were quick.

Freddie: It doesn't take long to milk a bull, does it! You think I'm daft or something? I can tell a cow's udder from a male thingummy.

Ralph: (*Grudgingly*) He wasn't scared... and Jester was in a filthy mood.

Betty: It's easy to be brave if you don't know something's dangerous.

Sheila: *Anyone* knows about bulls being fierce. Freddie knew, and he wasn't scared. And if you really thought I'd fall for taking a mad pig for a walk, you need your head examined.

Betty:	So how come you're covered in muck?
Freddie:	She got knocked over. Satisfied?
Betty:	You never went near her!
Ralph:	She did.
Sheila:	We were getting on like a house on fire till then. I'd better go and wash.
	(*Sheila exits.*)
Ralph:	Can I see your planes, Fred?
Freddie:	OK. Let's see what you've got.
	(*Betty watches the boys disdainfully.*)

Ralph: Crikey! Where did you get all those?

Freddie: I made the <u>Spitfires</u>. Swapped those <u>Hurricanes</u>... Bought that one... Mr Bing made the <u>Wellington</u>, he's a smashing handyman at the orph... the awful place I found...

Ralph: What's all this muck?

Freddie: Shrapnel. Had to leave most of it behind. I had stacks.

Ralph: Where'd you get it?

Freddie: Picked it up after raids. It comes down like metal hail stones. You find bits off planes too, flack, wheels, all sorts of junk.

Ralph: You lucky thing, seeing it all. Action! Hearing those bombers thrum-thrum-thrum up the river like you said...

Freddie: (*Sarcastically*) Yeah. I've been lucky all my life.

Ralph: I wouldn't have gone in a shelter. I'd stay to watch!

Freddie: You think so?

Ralph: And I'd lie about my age and join up if I could.

Betty: You'd have to grow about a yard taller first.

Ralph: So I'm growing! I don't get shorter! Girls! Come on, Fred, let's have a fight!

(*Ralph picks up some planes and makes bombing noises – wheeee-bang, P-chow! etc.*)

Ralph: Come on, Freddie! Fight back!

Spitfire: British fighter plane. Hurricane: British fighter plane.
Wellington: British light bomber.

Freddie: Forget it.

Betty: He's sulking. It's only a game, Fred.

Freddie: (*Sarcastically*) 'Course it is. Great fun.

Ralph: All right. Show me how it is for real.

(*A pause.*)

Freddie: You're the Germans. Get your bombers in formation…

Ralph: Like that?

Freddie: Further apart. Where's your fighter escort?

Ralph: Messerschmitts here, Junkers there?

Freddie: OK. This zig-zag bit on the carpet's a river. The red splodgy bits are targets. Y'know, docks, warehouses, gas, water supplies, railway stations…

Ralph: I'm coming in to bomb… (*He makes a growling sound.*) That the right noise?

Freddie: No. It's more like this… Come in low, bring your escort down.

Ralph: Bombs away!

Freddie: You're not supposed to enjoy being German!

Betty: Which of you is us?

Freddie: I'm us. Coming now… See?

Betty: Not much of a game, letting Ralph win. He's got more planes.

Freddie: That's the way it is, Betty. Our pilots are fighting back, but...

Betty: You're saying... Hitler's *winning*?

Ralph: 'Course he's not!

(*A pause.*)

Ralph: Is he?

Freddie: Well, no. But since France fell, the Germans have got closer. So we've got to win in the air. *Got* to, to stop them invading us.

Betty: You trying to scare us?

Ralph: Betty, shut up! Come on, Freddie, I'm on your tail.

Freddie: (*Suddenly playing earnestly*) Watch out! Spits coming from above. Ha! Didn't expect that, did you? There's one going down in flames... And another! I'm chasing your bomber...

Ralph: I'm offloading my bombs... Oh-oh! Bad luck, Cardiff!

Freddie: I'm on his tail... chasing him out to sea... Got him! I got him! There he goes, slap into the sea... SMASH! Oh boy!

Ralph: You didn't see my <u>Heinkel</u>... Hah! Now!

(*Excited fighting sounds. Martin and Joan come in.*)

Martin: (*Hoarsely*) Stop it! Stop all this.

Betty: They're just... Martin?

Martin: (*Kicking planes about in fury*) You stupid, stupid, *stupid*...

Ralph: Hey, steady, Martin! Joan, what's got into him?

Heinkel: German light bomber.

(Martin rushes out, sobbing harshly.)

Joan: *(Very calm)* We just had a telegram. Daddy's... Daddy's troop ship's been torpedoed. There aren't many... many survivors. We don't know...

(Betty stands, staring. Freddie goes to Joan and hugs her. She starts to cry.)

Freddie: I'm sorry. I'm sorry, sorry...

SCENE 6

The sitting room, later the same day. Sheila is painting, Freddie is mending his planes.

Freddie: (*Looking at Sheila's painting*) What the heck's *that*?

Sheila: The farm! Look – Betty being gored to death by Jester.

Freddie: You bloodthirsty thing! All the same... (*He laughs.*)

Sheila: Freddie... I've been thinking.

Freddie: Oh yes? What with?

Sheila: Seriously. When... *when* the war's over we'll be older.

Freddie: Maybe a lot older.

Sheila: And if Ma Blue's not there... and even if she is...

Freddie: They'll find somewhere for us. Don't worry, Sheila.

Sheila: *Two* somewheres. One for boys and one for girls. They do that.

Freddie: Well, I won't let them! Sheila, I swear it, I'll never let *anyone* split us up!

(Martin and Joan come in. There is an embarrassed atmosphere.)

Sheila: *(To Joan)* Here! I drew you a picture of the farm.

Joan: Thanks. What a sweet cow. You are kind.

Martin: Our mother's coming at the weekend...

Freddie: That'll be nice. I mean... nice for you...

Sheila: Oh look! Ralph's driving the tractor.

Joan: So he is.

Freddie: I'm going to clean out the dugout. I saw some boards, we could make a proper floor and it wouldn't be so damp. Coming, Martin?

(Martin looks at Joan anxiously. She shrugs.)

Martin: Yes. Good idea.

(Freddie and Martin exit. Joan sniffles miserably.)

Sheila: Joan... I'm ever so sorry about your dad. But they do pick up lots of survivors. Boatloads. 'Specially from troop ships.

Joan: Do they? Do they really?

Sheila: I saw it on a newsreel. Cross my heart. There's always hope.

Joan: Thanks, Sheila. *(Shakily)* I'm glad you're here.

Sheila: Well, we're both cuckoos in this nest, might as well be mates.

(Joan nods. There is an awkward silence.)

Joan: Sheila, you know what you said about your parents?

Sheila: What about them?

Joan: It wasn't true, was it? You can tell me.

Sheila: (*Suddenly*) I think Freddie's gone without his gas mask.

Joan: No, I saw him take it. Sheila?

Sheila: I don't know what you're talking about! Want to play ludo?

Joan: Mrs Green told me...

Sheila: She never! She promised she wouldn't!

Joan: She did it to cheer me up about Daddy. She said... oh, something like, "Just think of Freddie and Sheila who don't have any family at all..." I promised her I wouldn't tell any of the others. And I won't. But why did you lie to us?

Sheila: You're not an orphan, are you? Oh! Sorry! I didn't...

(Betty comes in unseen.)

Joan: Being an orphan's nothing to be ashamed of...

Sheila: It was in our school. They'd point us out. The orphans. Like we were guttersnipes no one wanted.

Joan: How cruel! I think you're very brave. Didn't you ever have any family at all?

Sheila: Freddie's my family. We've adopted each other.

(They laugh.)

Sheila: *(Confiding)* My mum and dad died in a fire. I can't remember them, so I can't miss them, can I?

Joan: Oh, Sheila... And Freddie?

Sheila: He was abandoned in a shop door. So that's it. Us. We've been in the same orphanage since we...

Betty: How touching. Little babes in the woods!

Joan: Betty! You sneak!

Sheila: How long have you been there?

Betty: Long enough. Just don't think you've found a fairy-tale ending and you can live here ever after! That's all.

(Betty goes out slamming the door. Shocked silence.)

Sheila: See? That's what being an orphan's like.

Joan: Ooh! The vicious, spiteful, mean...

Sheila: It doesn't bother me.

Joan: Jealous cat, I could strangle her!

(*Ralph and Freddie come in excitedly. Martin follows, subdued.*)

Ralph: There was a raid last night! They tried to bomb the <u>munitions dump</u> at Folksdown!

Joan: That's only four miles away!

Ralph: They used our river as a flight path. But they missed the dump and hit some houses and the jam factory!

Martin: People got killed. You don't have to make it sound like an adventure story!

Munitions dump: Store of ammunition.

Sheila: They'll come back. (*To Freddie*) Won't they?

Freddie: More than likely. It's still burning, so they've got a target.

Ralph: Then there's the station, the gas works, the...

Joan: Oh, stop!

Ralph: My dad's been there all night, leading the firefighters. He's still there. And Mum's gone to help the people who've been bombed out.

(*The sound of a siren.*)

Sheila: The shelter... come on. *Hurry.* Joan! Get your gas mask...

Ralph: Come on... Where's Betty? Run for it!

Scene 7

The dugout, evening. The children are all waiting impatiently for the all-clear.

Betty: I'm sick of this. I should be shutting the chickens up as Mum's not here.

Ralph: Wish I was firewatching with Dad. Open the door, I'm going.

Freddie: Don't! The light!

Martin: This is getting stupid... You said they were our planes that went over... <u>Blenheims</u> and Hurricanes.

Sheila: If Freddie said they were, they were!

Ralph: Well then, it's OK to go and... Blimey!

(*There is a heavy thrum-thrum of bombers, then fighter sounds.*)

Ralph: Freddie?

Blenheim: British light bomber.

Freddie: <u>Dorniers</u>! Cripes! It must be a massive formation!

Betty: I don't like it. I wish Mum and Dad were here.

Martin: Shut up. What's that other noise?

Freddie: Fighters. Could be their new Heinkel.

Joan: Good thing you kept the door shut.

Freddie: Come on! Where's our Ack-Ack? There should be a squadron of our fighters by now...

(*Ack-Ack starts.*)

Ralph: Fred?

Freddie: Hurricanes must have turned back...

(*Noise of fighting, planes, distant thuds etc.*)

Martin: What's happening? What's going on?

Freddie: I'm not flippin' up there, am I?

(*An enormous thud. Joan screams.*)

Betty: Was that a bomb?

Sheila: They don't drop teddy bears.

Betty: Oh no! Mum! Dad!

Ralph: It was miles away. Wasn't it, Fred? Tell her.

Joan: Was it? Was it?

Sheila: Yes! Wait. Listen...

(*Sound goes away. Silence.*)

Dornier: German bomber.

Martin: There you are. They've gone!

(*Ralph goes to the door and opens it a crack.*)

Ralph: There's a fire! The horses... It's near the stables!

Freddie: Come back! You can't go.

Betty: He's got to see to the animals!

Freddie: Not now! Martin! Help me. Stop him.

(*Martin and Freddie scuffle with Ralph and hold him down.*)

Freddie: Now shut up and listen! That fire's a target!

Ralph: The horses! Jester! Maureen! The cows...

Sheila: Listen, Ralph. Listen...

Betty: I can't stand it! I can't. Do something, someone!

Joan: Betty, calm down and belt up!

(*There is another, louder thump outside. Ralph breaks away and gets out. Freddie shuts the door.*)

Betty: Ralph! Go after him, Martin! Go on!

Sheila: No! You can't.

Martin: I can't hear any bombs.

Sheila: You don't hear the one that hits you.

Joan: But Ralph's out there!

Freddie: We can't help him now. Wait. Just wait.

(*More thumps.*)

Freddie: That's shrapnel.

Betty: Murderer! You murderer. Go after Ralph. Let me go!

Freddie: Stay there! Sheila, sit on her!

(*Martin, Sheila, Betty and Joan huddle together panicking. Freddie sneaks out. The panic subsides.*)

Martin: It's getting hot in here.

Betty: Not fair... Bombing harmless animals.

Joan: They should have shelters.

Sheila: No. They're better taking their chances in the open.

Martin: What's happening now? Where's Freddie?

Sheila: Having a look out. Anyone want a toffee?

Betty: I'm scared. Look out, Sheila. See if...

Sheila: No. We're safe in here.

Betty: It's all right for you.

Sheila: Oh, is it?

Martin: Shouldn't I go and see...

Joan: No! Stay with us!

Betty: I'm suffocating!

Sheila: They've gone over. Shrapnel's stopped. I'll have a look-see. (*She opens door.*) Oh my goodness!

(*Sheila rushes out.*)

Martin: What? Where's she going? Sheila?

Joan: Martin, you stay here... There's no point...

Betty: I wouldn't go out there for anything.

(Pause. Sighs, Shudders. Quiet outside.)

Martin: Someone's coming...

(Sheila comes in, supporting Ralph. He is bleeding and looks shattered. Betty screams.)

Betty: He's been hit! Ralph!

Ralph: *(Puffing)* Fell... barbed wire... Ouch... done my ankle...

Martin: What's happened? What's burning?

Ralph: Something landed by the stables.

Betty: The horses?

Sheila: Fine. Freddie got them out. They shot off up the hill.

Ralph: Fire engine's coming. Dad must have seen...

(Freddie comes in quietly, smoke-blackened.)

Joan: You all right?

Freddie: Think so. An incendiary set the stables alight.

Betty: The cows?

Freddie: The field's OK, the dogs are up there. Load of shrapnel fell in the yard. 'Fraid a lot of chickens are dead.

Ralph: Now what?

Sheila: Wait for the all-clear. You sure you're OK?

Ralph: Cuts and bruises... Good thing no one came after me. They'd have copped it.

Joan: We tried to. Freddie stopped us.

Betty: Yes. He did. And he's saved the horses...

Martin: Freddie did everything. I just sat here with the girls!

Joan: Isn't it quiet now? Is it really over?

Ralph: Who knows? Gosh, I'm hungry. We didn't have supper.

Martin: Sheila's got some toffees. Pass them round.

(*A pause.*)

Betty: Sorry I made such a fuss.

Sheila: Forget it.

Betty: (*Aside to Sheila*) And sorry for what I said about you being orphans and not staying here.

Martin: Orphans? Who's an orphan?

(*An uneasy pause.*)

Sheila: We are. Freddie and me.

Martin: But you said your parents were...

Freddie: That was a joke.

Joan: It's not funny! (*Earnestly to Ralph and Martin*) Neither of them have ever had a family, just each other. And they're so brave...

Sheila: Don't blub again! You'll flood the dugout!

Betty: Oh heck! And I've been so vile to you both! And now... now...

Sheila: Oh, forget it. Don't you start crying as well!

(*The all-clear sounds. They look at each other.*)

Ralph: Well? Better go and see the damage.

Martin: I'll help sort out the chickens.

Betty: I'll go and get those poor dogs in. They'll be terrified. Could you... would you come and help me, Sheila?

Sheila: OK.

Joan: It'll be horrible out there.

Ralph: It is. We'll just have to start getting used to it. The war's come to all of us now.